TO WAKE TO THIS

First published in 2009 by
The Dedalus Press
13 Moyclare Road
Baldoyle
Dublin 13
Ireland

www.dedaluspress.com

Editor: Pat Boran

ISBN 978 1 906614 11 9

Dedalus Press titles are represented in North America
by Syracuse University Press, Inc., 621 Skytop Road,
Suite 110, Syracuse, New York 13244, and in the UK by
Central Books, 99 Wallis Road, London E9 5LN

Cover image 'Clooncunny, Roscommon' copyright © Peter Sirr

The Dedalus Press receives financial assistance from
The Arts Council / An Chomhairle Ealaíon

TO WAKE TO THIS

To Dell —
Baby Jesus in my
Argus!
Enda Wyley *thanks for*
coming to my
reading at Merrion.
Love Enda
Aug 2014

DEDALUS PRESS
DUBLIN, IRELAND

ACKNOWLEDGEMENTS

Acknowledgements are due to the editors of the following in which a number of these poems originally appeared:

The Irish Times, PN Review, Agenda, Oxford Magazine, The Warwick Review, The Echoing Years (Anthology of Canadian and Irish Poetry, Newfoundland), *Sunday Miscellany 2004-2006* and *Sunday Miscellany 2006-2008 (ed. Cliodhna Ní Anluain), Southword, The Best of Irish Poetry 2008* (ed. Thomas McCarthy), *The Best of Irish Poetry 2009* (ed. Paul Perry), *Wingspan: A Dedalus Sampler* (2006, ed. Pat Boran) and *Poetry Europe / Europoésie* (2009, ed. John F. Deane).

I am indebted to The Arts Council / An Chomhairle Ealaíon for Bursaries received in Literature 2005 and 2008.

For Lynda Mulvin and Revati Daisy

&

Peter and Freya Sirr

Contents

Part One

Little Heart

for Freya

In your folds tonight
are strawberries
to wash away,
some knots of tuna
netted there,
and up along
your neckline
sweet corn beads
that make
a precious chain.

In your head
the dog is barking
and the small wall clock
is gently ticking,
your tongue clicking
to its time.
Little heart
not yet hurt,
beat on.

Twelve Days

Twelve days you've been gone.
My hands swell in the heat of loss;
in the heat of where you are—
the slow, soupy air of Buenos Aires—tapping
its grid system with your fingertips you map
your way home down the long jacaranda avenues.

We hear traffic noise, a fountain, children shrieking.
Here you are a shadow in our heads, a voice lost
in our ears, a face fading on the computer screen.
How can I say what I mean, just how it really is?
The dog is nuzzling into our sheets, the smell of you
still there, and I can't dream without you. Come home.

Bird

for my mother

Whoever says the world
cannot be stilled
by a bird
has not been here
in this dark gallery,
nor knelt on the late
afternoon floor
and gently pulled
frames forward,
seen images
speeding by
like the old flick books
we loved as children—
the head of a dead poet,
those dark shawls
of Markey's women
in the West.
Until suddenly
your world
is stilled
by this bird—
quirky, tufted thing
proud in charcoal,
flown over forty years
from studio to home
and now landed
in this city gallery.
So faded is the wood
that frames him,

and his cover
is such chipped
and mottled glass.
And yet your world
is stilled by this bird
that flapped from
Jan de Fouw's hand
when you were young
with your small children
and did not know how
you would make it to here
or that this bird would fly
forever in search of you,
his head flung westward,
his speckled heart beating
until there is nothing left
but you and the bird—
quirky, tufted thing
that stills this place.

To Wake to This

If we had known
we would not
have slept so long.
Mist has fought and won
its battle against the sun
and all is murky grey.
The spider's frail line blows
from the sycamore
to the cottage hedge,
while across the lane
dew looks dense but breaks
like bubbles at a touch.
The fat brown birds
are not afraid of our steps
along the gravelled way,
of our fingers
squeezing berries.
Oh purple hunger!
The baby dips
in and out of wonder,
twirling the soft air,
testing the sky
with her sounds.
Geraniums wake bedraggled
in their window beds
and yesterday's paint dries
at last on the red wooden door.
To wake to this.

Lucky

Lucky the man
who listens
to Monteverdi,
who walks
out the quiet lane,
Lamento della Ninfa
in his head, and finds
the hedgerow yellow
with wild primrose,
the stones a maze
for the spider, the fields
undulating with ewes
and their soot-faced
soot-eared young.

Lucky the man who
hears the pheasant rising
high over Hunt's field
and is startled as much by it
as by the tenor
singing in soprano
the poem of another man
writing as a woman
in the seventeenth century—
contradictions
complex and beautiful,
like dust-mites he sees
falling down now
through the sun's rays.

This That Is

1.

This that is
still
and is
to others
just a lane
with a lake below
and a sun falling above it—

that is
just high grass
with secrets of ticks,
frogs, the odd lizard—
is to us this and more:
a field rising

with tractor marks
after the cut hay,
wild geese, their necks
towards Beatrice's house,
its avenue and many rooms,
all her children gone,

but us still here
in this stillness
we've found
by accident
and are slow to let go of.
How can we?

Even the wagtails
find a nest
under the eaves
of this place
and will not leave.
We copy them—
see blackness fall
against the sash windows,
giant moths press to the glass,
the full moon rise over Hunt's
and love what others do not know—
this stillness.

2.

This morning
this window
to stare out of
from the edge
of our bed
with you—
your little feet
dangling,
your mouth
half-opened
as though ready
to gulp down whole
each blue-tit
that we know
will soon flit
from our eaves,
all cheeky bravery
nested there.

This minute
that is still
and is ours,
framed by
the cottage window,
the high grass beyond
whispering secrets
that only
the future can know.
But for now
we are happy
there is this bed,
this morning,
this window,
these blue-tits
to wait for—
and you.

Clooncunny

How our hands swayed through
reeds today, brushing against joy—
the curlew calling us on in single file,
the others back in the cottage and us free,
marvelling at how we'd come this far, our voices
rising clear along the soggy path to the jetty,
the lake rippling with rudd and perch.
What comes next we can only guess,
can only wonder at where we are now,
at the top of this green, sloping field,
the quiet inside of us growing.

Gold Wallpaper

The night was ours—
young art students clambering up cathedral hills,
not afraid to force a window open, creak a door
inwards, brush cobwebs like a gasp of cold air
from our cheeks.

We were finding old houses
to make paintings in—you, a corner of shadows
to place your easel near, while I spent evenings
sketching the way starlight fell through cracked
glass and how the bone moon creaked.

Over ancient wooden floors,
ice-blue marble mantelpieces, the dusty mattresses
with the dent of those long gone still there,
the yellow light crept, a ghost across our canvases.
Old houses forgotten by all but us.

On and on we'd wander
up avenues swirling their yew tree spells,
scraping our knees and notebooks on the forbidden
chipped sills, our pencils and brushes scraping for life
while the city below slept.

Until in one crumbling mansion,
your fingers touched mine and from the thick walls
fat with damp we stripped back seventies swirls,
sixties floral patterns, the formal fifties lines—
and found gold.

Gold wallpaper lanterns and flowers trailing
delicate stems and light up to the shattered cherubs,
the intricate cornices, the tinkling, blackened chandeliers.
So beautiful we could not paint that night—
but held hands and stared and stared.

Even now in the hush of our own home,
in the dark of our middle years, when you turn
from me in sleep, your mouth muttering dreams
I cannot know, I reach for your skin—

gold paper falling onto me from you.

Sea Urchin

after Rachel Joynt's sculpture, 'The Mothership', Dun Laoghaire

Summer came and we dived from the sea path
like feeding terns onto the granite rocks.
Bladderwrack, barnacles, crabs—our after-school prey;
above us, our parents staring out over Scotsman's Bay.

We had rubber-clad feet, buckets as bags, we were cruel
and carefree, stuck sticks into the deep red anemone,
yanked sea sprats from their warm rock-pool worlds,
pierced winkles with sewing needles and did not care.

Then from the sandy-bottomed waters the seals rose,
their sleekness a soft oil poured over our clamour,
and we were soothed into stillness, perched ourselves
close to the cormorants drying their outstretched feathers.

Now just there, across the path, silver droplets stream
from the sculptor's shell—a bronze-cast sea urchin turned
on its side, like an ear hoarding the sea's roar,
a cave full of children's cries, echoes of what we were

before St Michael's church burnt to the ground,
the great black birds had all flown south, the baths
grown derelict—before we ever knew the bogeyman
might come, to chase us home along The Metals.

* The Metals, now a laneway, was the old railway line built in the 19th century to
deliver granite from Dalkey Quarry to Dun Laoghaire to build the pier.

Strange Things in Strange Places

for the sculptor Janet Mullarney, Magione Tower, Umbria

Go up the tower steps and find
strange things in strange places—
your red dog, old devil, clawing
a space on a crocheted shawl
high over the first stone floor,
knee-high blue men standing
in a row, who welcome beasts
and birds on their shoulders—
their skulls knots of creatures
jutting out towards the magic sun
and battlements of Magione.

The head of another beast
sticks out from the side of a bell jar,
nudges us down steps, out to a still night.
We stand on a hill over the red-roofed town,
the cypress trees and ridged, brown land.
Our giant shadows flap from the light
of the tower to its tiny top window,
then they clamber back inside, leaving
our real selves, bereft of strange things,
stumbling down alleys to a meal
to which the host will never come.

Postcard

for Peter Porter

You have been to Norfolk
and Hampshire—
then Pays de Cathare,
near Carcassonne.

*How odd that massacres
eight hundred years old
are now tourist themes!*

You are on a train
northeast of Toulouse,
your day dwarfed
by Albi's cathedral.
Now your heart
is the flamboyant south portal,
you feel light as the lace rood screen,
your thoughts are a nave
of enormous proportions,
each second an abundance of frippery—
then Eve, like love, tugs you
to the central door.

Outside, there is the river,
the covered passages,
the little square,
the road to Cordes—
and your postcard
beating upwards like a bird
with its wings spread north.

Caitlín Maude Sings on the Radio

Caitlín Maude sings on the radio
and you upstairs, busy fingering sleep
like a button on your night cardigan,
tossing nightmares aside
with a shake of your hot head,
are suddenly alert to the downstairs song,
raise your head to sing in tune with her—
black-haired bard long dead,
still clear-pitched, rhythmical, true.

Room

after Nuala O'Faoláin

Saddest of all,
to leave behind
this room.
It isn't its fault
that I have to go
and yet these days
I hate it.
It is everything
I will lose,
everything I know
there is not—
the heaven
I will never reach,
the air I will
no longer breathe,
all my memory
blanked out.
How can I
leave it now?
I press my back
against its door,
block its edges
with old cloths,
socks and towels,
yet still the light
creeps through,
burns my heels
and finger-tips—
taunts me with
tomorrow.

Work's Hard

after Cesare Pavese's 'Lavorare Stanca'

This afternoon a man
is sweeping
below my window,
though I cannot see him,
only hear
the gentle brush of earth
from the road's centre
into a metal skip—
and I think
of someone's garden
flattened for winter planting,
the lane before it open-gated
sprinkled with soil trails,
tufts of green, panicked insects.

From where I am,
the cherry blossom
is red and orange constancy,
its trunk sturdy
as the lamp post.
Near its twitching leaves
a street wire slants—
while on tiled roofs
over red walls,
the chimney tops lean.

This sun is hard,
this work is hard.
The man's face

turns to his mate.
They are shovelling
mounds of soil now
onto the pile already there,
their faces lined from days
of weather like this.
Cars and trucks
are a whirling ocean
drowning their voices,
an aeroplane hums
like a dull afternoon.
I cannot hear
what they say now,
these men clambering
into their vans,
dirt in their finger-nails,
heading for pints
in their local pub,
while outside two pigeons
fall from the window sill
and below on the street
a man going home sighs,
Work's hard, this sun is hard.

View from a Bus

1.

From the upper deck,
I suddenly see you both—
father and daughter
below on the street—
passing the high houses,
the dirty railings,
the difficult intersections,
and my face presses
against the window.

How I want to be with you—
to nuzzle into her skin,
make her ours all over.
But the bus moves on
and I stare behind.
Back there, the two of you
wait at the traffic lights,
each so strongly there—
then are gone from me
in a moment.

2.

Today I saw the other you—
taller, younger, slimmer.
It was as if you had walked
out to me from the glow
of a summer's day years ago
and I was seeing you
again for the first time.
The whole of the street
was your friend.
I saw how you waved
and smiled at everyone,
how their icy breath warmed.

By the corner of the avenue
you stood handsome
as those sycamore trees
I have always loved
and your voice rose
in many languages.
I jumped from the bus,
passed close to you
and felt your hand
brush mine so slightly—
feathers, silk, petals
against my skin.
Then you moved
effortlessly on
and were gone,
without me
ever knowing
the other you.

White

1.

White sheets
on a white bed,
the slow tick
of Sunday light,
leaves beating
on the dusty window.
Before, there was
too much noise,
too much clatter
but now this peace,
like the trill of a bird,
a flutter of something
new in my pulse,
a door pushing out,
somebody calling.

2.

There is only whiteness now:
white sheets; white pillows
on a flat futon; white from a moon
over Francis Street
and Harry Clarke's stained-glass
full of a ghostly Christ hanging;
white light from the spying
parish priest's window
as we pace about this flat
in our own whiteness
over red houses, cobblestones.
We are white in our deep good-bye
before the streets of Dublin change—
and late-night horses from Smithfield
are the only dull recognition of life.

Bully's Acre

Royal Hospital, Kilmainham

We stand at Bully's Acre,
the old gates chained.
Beyond, the trees are vast,
the gardener's work
a full circle of cut grass
smooth as a blanket,
around the trunks' base.

At evening
the snatched bodies
from centuries ago
will rise from the surgeons'
ancient slabs,
retreat to their graves again
and we will find home in each other—
Bully's Acre with gates thrown wide.

Notebook Shop

All the poems we might write,
gather here in these blank books
made from vellum, soft indian paper,
shelved in the corner shop on Francis Street.
But then a wind blows the door open,
the bell rings, and our thoughts float
out and up past the antique shops,
the Tivoli Theatre pounding its heart
of rehearsals, Oxfam's sofa graveyard
and the man from the Coombe
clattering by with his horse and cart—
our unmade poems coming alive,
flapping on the seagulls' wings,
peeping into the cages of Marsh's library,
singing with St Patrick's choir,
lying down in St Werburgh's
with Edward Fitzgerald and Major Sirr.
There is no end to where our poems go—
anywhere to be free, not to be trapped
in these fine and beautiful books
that are hungry for a scribble,
a dream, the rush of a word.

Part Two

The Page Within

We write for the page within,
the unexpected beat
like the baby's trace
in the hospital today—
spidery mountains squirming
free of the monitor
with each speedy thump
of the heart inside,
fluid roaring like elephants
or the whirl of water all around
when snorkelling deep, deep down.

We write for all these things
and later, the slow, stiff recovery,
foolishly small-stepping
behind the mad-cap dog's ways,
every gate post, street lamp
his to make his own.
Even the glass on Carlisle Street
from last night's stolen car
is his treasure to sniff at
in the blue evening light.
And the baby ripples within,
and this page that fills is filling fast.

Saturday Poem

'… this blessing love gives again into our arms.'
—*Galway Kinnell*

I would rather curl, still groggy,
sleepy-eyed and dressing-gowned
back into the blue-striped crumples
of last night's sleep,
smell yesterday in your hair,
see the white stains
of your open-mouthed dreams
like tiny footprints mounting
the pillow's feathers.

But you play Galway Kinnell
for me, his little boy padding
out from the computer speaker
dressed in baseball pyjamas,
wanting to snuggle and hug us
to giggle and play.
I am wide awake.
Our own child is a mouse
in a cupboard, a pulse, a ripple,
a sudden shift of life
under my skin where
the soft belly hairs have grown
so far, for thirty-seven weeks.

We lie down, my stomach
against yours, see the rain outside
wash our newly painted sills,
the marigolds' orange mouths,
and let this poem's child be
our child's first friend,
then celebrate the words
we are lucky to hear
with a breakfast of pancakes
fat with apples, plums, a pear.

Diary

1.

In the room we get ready for you,
books are scattered everywhere—
and there are other things too,
like the cracked terracotta pot,
a dusty old glasses case, one container
of printer ink, the wobbly wooden chair.
I look and look, get used to these things
we should tidy away, to clear our life up,
as though you are a visitor we must prepare for.

You—a floating fish,
a blip-blipping in my fluid,
a force that aches in my lower back,
a twitch below my appendix mark,
the plucking of fingers inside of me.
You will make music in my blood,
burst into our life
that is already yours.
So lie back with me, little one,
in the pale sheets of our waiting.
Maybe, just for now,
I'll leave things as they are—
those dusty, cracked, scattered pieces
of what we have become—
and let your new life nestle between us,
beneath my skin.

2.

You are here. What can I say
but that you are everything
I knew you'd be.
You are someone
I have always known.
You have never not been here.
And how definite you are
after just a few short weeks on this earth.
You do not take things lightly—
stare at everything,
wide-eyed, frowning.
And when your eyes catch the light,
a deep chuckle shakes your body.
Then I am happy.
Then I lift you in my hands
and hold you flat over my head—
you squealing in delight.
When I nuzzle into your stomach,
you clutch at my hair and won't let go.
They are the moments
before the dog barks at a cat
and scares you, or a sudden wind
makes you cry.
Why should I worry
about anything anymore?
You are here.

3.

Under my pillow tonight,
your yellow and turquoise giraffe.
All day I watched you with this,
twirling it between your tiny hands
like magic thread—
fascinated by every sound
this bright thing made,
every look it cast your way.
Then when you got too tired,
you closed your eyes on it and us.
In the morning, you will stretch
for the soft, tinkling ball,
the bright cloth storybook,
the doll with the mad string hair
and forget about the giraffe.
You have other things to find, explore—
like my hand in yours, the straps of my dress,
your father's bristly skin, our eyes.

4.

There are late-night and early-morning feeds.
They dig black circles below my eyes
and my sleep shortens
with your shuffling,
your opening eyes.
Now I must stumble to attention.
I am the waking dead,
pushing a tomb-stone aside,
pulling you out and up
from your basket warmth.
I fumble with buttons,
and milk speeds
like lightening
through my breasts.
I fill your mouth with me.

5.

Most beautiful when you wake,
you come to me resisting food
as you did sleep hours before,
your fingers a web of energy,
your face a thousand knots,
your skin blotched with the stains
of just being alive—
the deep-cut mark
above your nose
where thinking has begun.
Oh, so much longing
brought you here.

Translating Brecht

for Peter

You have been in the market
with him all month.
Nobody remembers him—
his friends, the woman
he slept with for years,
all walk right past him
or just nod politely.
He is a stranger to his own life.
Even his clothes
hanging from the line in his yard
have changed.
They are faded, patched, misshapen.
Somebody else
has been living his life in them.

But how can you say
all this clearly?
You slip into his words
awkwardly,
a stranger adjusting
another's thoughts,
trying to make them your own—
slip German from his world,
scatter English on the page.

And all the while she rests,
her tiny head below your chin,
her fingers clutching
the top of your shirt

as though it were a rope, lowering
her down to sleep, her eyes rolling
into the whiteness of her dreams.
She squirms into your warmth,
asking to be held, to be made sense of.

Night Guard

When I get home you are upstairs,
standing on the landing,
your huge book
a block of pale corn-light
wedged between your fingers,
your eyes squinting in the gloom,
your mind so fixed on Borges' words
that you don't hear me there at all,
breathing close to the turn of the stair,
watching how it must be sometimes
when I am away from you and her.

It is late and you shoulder presses
into the frame of her nursery door
as though holding it solidly in place,
your hip like a firm nail in its side.
One socked foot presses on the other
casually, yet I know you would easily
jump into action if needed
because you are her night guard.
Intense reader but alert to every breath,
each restless move, all her tiny cries,
those early fears that populate the dark.

She has curled herself into a drowsy ball,
her fists tight under her hot belly,
her bottom to the air, one side of her face
gone pink in the furious stream of sleep,
turned away from the day she's left behind
dishevelled, well-worn, like her minute clothes
flung on the creaking wooden floor.

Up on her wall the clock's fairy dreams
on a bed of strawberries, and from where I am
time can be heard *ticking* and *tocking* and then
becoming your loyal pulse beating just for her.

Magpie

The day builds itself piece by piece;
the newt joins the owl, then the porcupine,
quince on its branch bends over a ruby ring,
colour seeping across the living room floor

until the jigsaw's yacht sails to its zebra end
and we go walking, your hand a small ball
in my palm poised to roll where adventure hides
in parks, wild gardens, up doorsteps, behind pots.

Your eyes, beady berries on Raymond Street's trees,
see everything—and then, just there, *muck-pie,*
muck-pie, you call to the bird that tussles
with the daffodils, that pecks for sparkling light

like diamonds through the railings. Our day
building and renewing will not stop.
Blueberries devoured, cod stew and sleep
the warm milk of waking, later the afternoon

becoming a city of wooden blocks up to the ceiling—
only the great moon in the sky and the twinkling star
will drag you in song from your industry.
Then night has you nestling close to my neck,

your lips whispering the day's things softly.
Muck-pie, muck-pie, your energy pulling
at the jade on my chain feels relentless to me—
like the jay all ready to steal and fly away.

Shadows and Reflections

Even when you're sick
you find shadows everywhere—
in the hall, or up on the ceiling
when the shadow of my head
is a wild monster
that night insects swarm to nip at,
or my hand becomes a long-fanged wolf
twirling, snarling at you.

And you are absorbed by reflections,
by that other world poised
in the old back door's pane
where a vague Moroccan plate
balances in the air,
or the dining room lamp
blurs on a table under the tree—
absurd reflections in the glass,
our inner room seeming outside.

All this looks strange—but not to you.
You are waving at your reflection out there
amongst the ghostly things, at your high chair
and you in it on top of the mossy cobblestones.
For that is the world through glass,
reflected as a blur, unreachable,
the life we know in unlikely positions.

You pat your hand on the window,
then I pull the red blind down.
Bye, bye, I say, *Bye, bye,*
your clammy hand a newly learnt wave,
your temperature dipping,
the pink on your cheeks a fever,
fading to a close at last.

Game

Into your sleep you fall.
I would go with you if I could,
where there is only your world—
a mother, a father, a dog,
a terraced house with a door
green as the holly tree that guards it,
a yard paved with our journey to here.
Jasmine and lavender catch
in the wheels of a bicycle,
a pram, or in the speedy twist
of your curious little hand;
a snail is relentless joy to hold;
a fallen branch is a wand of spells;
the door opens to us lounging
on sheets of cotton, the bed
forever blue as your eyes now
staring into mine unblinking.
'It's a game,' you say, 'I've won.'
My eyes closing, then opening to you.

Trees that Lead to You

Sycamore, copper beech, oak,
steadfast on Adelaide Road
one winter afternoon—
these trees that lead to you

flinging your day into my arms,
your face at last close to mine,
the hour before tea and the night
that sneaks you away from me again.

In your bag a handmade mask
burns orange as the toppling sun,
You've been hours away from me
and your shirt is a muddy testament to fun.

At the steps of the church the rector
pins his dream to the notice board.
We stand beneath these trees.
Fear not. Only love can lead to You.

The White Witch Will Come

'And yes,' I said,
'She will come,
spreading ice
on our foolish moods,
the entire city
frozen,
the wardrobe
becoming
our whole new life,
us pressing
into snow
and lampposts,
the noble lion's
bloodied mane.'

'Don't ever
say that again!'
you cried.
Little one,
younger
but stronger
than me,
less cruel;
already your skin
is a sheath
of unbreakable ice
and through the sky—
look, come closer!—
a chariot of snow
is speeding near.

First Words

Tongue on her palette
and a horse gallops
into the room,
then a story cat
leaps from her mouth,
meow, meow, meow...
breakfast jam smudges
on the page
and a morning bird
is a tweet on her lips.
We hear rain, *shhh...*
see her soft tumble
down to the Marakech rug.
There's *Oh deah,* when things scatter,
clatter, fall apart at her wild touch,
mwah is a wide, moist mouth
open on our cheeks
at the end of the day,
oh a plate piled
with steaming supper.
Even in sleep
she still practices.
We tiptoe down stairs,
hear through the night monitor
whispers start up again—
meow, ssh, deah, mwah—
secret lullabies from her to us.

Talisman

First the jade,
pure circle of stone
trimmed with fine gold,
swung on a thin chain.
Then the skin-smooth agate
that you dropped
in the Departures lounge
and was lost
one May day
in Chicago
when we were rushing
between worlds.
Now a fever runs
through you,
and you are a fire
in our arms,
screeching,
unquenchable,
your head drenched
with late-night sweats,
your mattress raised,
the steaming bowl
moistening the air
with eucalyptus.
In your fist
the rose quartz cools.
After, we cleanse it
in sea salt and water:
this precious stone
that rolls your sickness
away from us

makes you forget it all,
search for what might be
beyond the yard's brambles,
beyond your talisman.

War

Because the world
is quiet here,
because you nod
your head in sleep,
because I can turn you over,
place another blanket
across your midriff,
because the moth lands
on our oatmeal carpet
and is still in darkness,
because the wind howls
but there are no gunshots,
because we do not have to
cross borders
to a new, raw life,
or run out of numbers
to count our dead—
because of all these things
we know we are lucky
to rest here in our home,
the others not forgotten,
their bodies battered,
their bloodied noses
barely touching.

Blessing

for Revati

To be kind—
to delve deep into the hearts
of those you despise
and find there the majesty of trees.

To be patient
with fear—
it will leave you
and you will be brave,

a child letting go
of its father's hand,
a bird cupped into the air
free ...

To love life
and be loved—because
the lived life is the loved life;
and so, love everything—

urban fox racing
up Montague Street,
perfect umbrella of leaves
shading a city yard,
the month of your birth,
the way light falls
on your mother's face
when she sees you
for the first time ...

You are newborn.
Your hair is a cloak
of dark sea birds,
your legs, tall rowan trees,

your mouth, a cluster
of red berries, your tiny voice
like gentle rain
wetting our lips with hope.

You have come into this earth,
a warm bundle of things we've forgotten.
Kindness, patience, courage
blesses us and you.

May your life be lived and loved.

Postcards

1.

Waking knotted together in sleep
we unwind one another—
threads freed into the day.

2.

In her hair I smell
my own childhood—
waft of a long ago Summer
on a cold February night.

3.

When you cry out *Meow, Meow,*
after dark when only the clock ticks
and the monitor sounds like a sea
in our room, are you dreaming of cats?

4.

Swallows break into the cold blue—
three perfect forks over The Sacred Heart
cased in glass at the top of O'Connell Street—
then cluster together, make for another time.

5.

After sleep,
you in my widening arms.
I waited for you,
I listened for you,
We are here.

Printed in the United Kingdom by
Lightning Source UK Ltd., Milton Keynes
142165UK00001B/44/P